Super Successful People Will Never Tell You That You Can't

Who Are You Hanging Out With?

By
Manny Nowak

Successful People Will Never Tell You That You Can't
Who Are You Hanging Out With?
Copyright © 2018 Manny Nowak
All rights reserved.

DEDICATION

This book is dedicated to my wife and partner for life. The one who has always helped me, encouraged me and backed me up, no matter how hard or tough or crazy it got.

Thank you Cheryl L. Nowak.

Also want to take this opportunity to thanks all those who helped me to make this book happen.

Special thanks to Elaine Starling for all her help in being a great accountability partner and helping me keep going in making this book a reality. Also for her help in reviewing and adding some excellent information along the way. Thank you Elaine.

Thanks to my clients who have been using the 90 days process, both formally and informally over many years. It has taken a great deal of trial and error to get it working as smooth and effectively as it is. It has helped many of them to move their businesses to new levels of success. But they have also helped me in being able to help so many more of you. Thank you.

Enjoy this book and may it help you to take your life to new levels of success. Coach Manny Nowak

manny@mannynowak.com

www.CoachManny.com

DISCLAIMER

ALL RIGHTS RESERVED. NO PART OF THIS BOOK MAY BE REPRODUCED IN ANY FORM WITHOUT PERMISSION IN WRITING FROM THE AUTHOR. REVIEWERS MAY QUOTE BRIEF PASSAGES IN REVIEWS. DISCLAIMER AND FTC NOTICE NO PART OF THIS PUBLICATION MAY BE REPRODUCED OR TRANSMITTED IN ANY FORM OR BY ANY MEANS, MECHANICAL OR ELECTRONIC, INCLUDING PHOTOCOPYING OR RECORDING, OR BY ANY INFORMATION STORAGE AND RETRIEVAL SYSTEM, OR TRANSMITTED BY EMAIL WITHOUT PERMISSION IN WRITING FROM THE PUBLISHER. WHILE ALL ATTEMPTS HAVE BEEN MADE TO VERIFY THE INFORMATION PROVIDED IN THIS PUBLICATION, NEITHER THE AUTHOR NOR THE PUBLISHER ASSUMES ANY RESPONSIBILITY FOR ERRORS, OMISSIONS, OR CONTRARY INTERPRETATIONS OF THE SUBJECT MATTER HEREIN. THIS BOOK IS FOR ENTERTAINMENT PURPOSES ONLY. THE VIEWS EXPRESSED ARE THOSE OF THE AUTHOR ALONE, AND SHOULD NOT BE TAKEN AS EXPERT INSTRUCTION OR COMMANDS. THE READER IS RESPONSIBLE FOR HIS OR HER OWN ACTIONS. ADHERENCE TO ALL APPLICABLE LAWS

AND REGULATIONS, INCLUDING INTERNATIONAL, FEDERAL, STATE, AND LOCAL GOVERNING PROFESSIONAL LICENSING, BUSINESS PRACTICES, ADVERTISING, AND ALL OTHER ASPECTS OF DOING BUSINESS IN THE US, CANADA, OR ANY OTHER JURISDICTION IS THE SOLE RESPONSIBILITY OF THE PURCHASER OR READER. NEITHER THE AUTHOR NOR THE PUBLISHER ASSUMES ANY RESPONSIBILITY OR LIABILITY WHATSOEVER ON THE BEHALF OF THE PURCHASER OR READER OF THESE MATERIALS. ANY PERCEIVED SLIGHT OF ANY INDIVIDUAL OR ORGANIZATION IS PURELY UNINTENTIONAL. I SOMETIMES USE AFFILIATE LINKS IN THE CONTENT. THIS MEANS IF YOU DECIDE TO MAKE A PURCHASE, I WILL GET A SALES COMMISSION. BUT THAT DOESN'T MEAN MY OPINION IS FOR SALE. EVERY AFFILIATE LINK ON IS TO PRODUCTS THAT I'VE PERSONALLY USED AND FOUND USEFUL. PLEASE DO YOUR OWN RESEARCH BEFORE MAKING ANY PURCHASE ONLINE.

Table of Contents

Introduction
Chapter 1   Who are you listening to
Chapter 2   You Are the Average of the 5 People You Spend the Most Time With
Chapter 3   The Few, The Proud, The Marines. USMC
Chapter 4   You Are Amazing
Chapter 5   Stop Limiting Yourself
Chapter 6   Never Put a limit on Your Dreams
Chapter 7   Stretch Yourself
Chapter 8   Remove Your Limits
Chapter 9   Opinions are like? – Everyone has one and they all stink.

Section 2   **3 Keys to Success**
Chapter 10   Vision
Chapter 11   Road to Success
Chapter 12   Your Why
Chapter 13   Plan
Chapter 14   Goals
Chapter 15   Stretch/10X
Chapter 16   Tasks
Chapter 17   Measurements.
Chapter 18   Accountability
Chapter 19   90 days to your success

Section 3   **Action is What makes it happen.**
Chapter 20   Persistence
Chapter 21   Discipline
Chapter 22   Morning routine
Chapter 23   Practice
Chapter 24   Listening
Chapter 25   One Final Story Adversity
Chapter 26   Conclusion

Introduction:

And do not be conformed to this world, but be transformed by the renewing of your mind, that you may prove what is that good and acceptable and perfect will of God.

Romans 12:2

Contentment is the greatest enemy of success.
Once content, people have no drive to move any further.

This book is about going for the gold.
God has given us so many talents and abilities, yet most people hardly touch the surface of all they could do if they used all their abilities.

There is a great story in the Bible that goes something like this:

The master was going on a journey and left all his money in the hands of 3 servants.
The first he gave five talents.
The second he gave two talents to.
Finally, he gave the third one talent.
Then he went away.
Years later he returned.

When he returned:
He asks the first servant how he has done?
He answered, "I took your five talents and now return 10 to you."
The master said, "well done my good and faithful servant."

Then he asks the second how he had done?
He answered, "I took your two talents and now return 4 to you."
The master said, "well done my good and faithful servant."

Then he came to the third servant and like the others, he asked how he did.
He answered, "all knew you were a very tough person and thus I was afraid. I took your talent and buried it so it would not get lost or stolen."

Then master then replied, "You are a bad servant, you did nothing with what I gave you. The least you could have done was put it in the bank and got interest."
So he took the talent from the servant and banished him from the kingdom.
Then he gave the talent to the one who already had 10.

The moral of the story.
Don't waste what God has given you.
Take it and use it and create great success.

This is what this book is all about.
Please read, enjoy and learn how to use your talents to the maximum.
This book follows the process of my keynote speech by the same name.

Chapter 1

Who Are You Listening to?

Speak Little, Do much.
Benjamin Franklin

Successful people will never tell you that "you can't."

So the question to each one of you today is, "Who are you listening to?"

Who are you listening to today and every day?

This is a question that each of you needs to take time and ask yourself – can you really answer it truthfully?

Who do I listen to?
Where are they in life?
How are they doing?
Where they are… is that where you want to be?
Really?
Are you sure?

If you don't like the answers that you are getting, then perhaps it is time to re-think the situation.

Chapter 1 Exercise:

1/ Make a list of those people you listen to.
    Be honest.
    Those that are influencing your life, like it or not.
    All that you can think of.

2/ Next to each name, write where they are in life and how they are doing.

3/ Then for each person on the list, ask yourself, is that really where you would like to be? Just a simple - Yes or No.

Afterward, take a look at your results.
Sadly, sometimes our list is mostly "no's."
But that is okay.
What you have just learned is that it is time to get a new crowd to hang with.
Don't take this lightly, it will influence the rest of your life.

You have to surround yourself with people who you want to be like.
Otherwise, you will become like the ones you are around.

Chapter 2.

You Are the Average of the 5 People You Spend The Most Time With

"So be bold and don't worry about what people think. They don't do it that often anyway."
4 Hour Work Week.

Let's look at very popular piece out there today, which I can remember my mom always telling me as a kid. In fact, growing up it was one of those things you heard all over the place. It was what parents always told their children.

"Don't hang out with "those" kids – they will just end up in trouble.
If they get in trouble, so will you."

But what if they are the only ones who will accept me? Especially those out there with that rebel personality. Many of whom today are the successful entrepreneurs.

For me, I did not listen to my mom. As I am sure many of the rest of you did not either.
So, I have been there and done that one.

I was raised to be a good kid by my mom.
My mom and dad came to this country before I was born. They were part of the people who were sponsored and brought into America to work at Seabrook Farms. They came from Austria and Romania.
They worked hard, buying some land to build a house on. Partnered with each other to work different shifts and take care of me.
On their way to the American dream.

Then my dad had a heart attack at 32 and died.
I was 2.

There was my mom was all alone in this country, but a tough lady who stayed here instead of doing what many would do, go back home.

I grew up in a home filled with love and a neighborhood that was a little tough.

But then came the year of being a teenager and the trouble began when I started hanging out with the wrong kids.

I ended up getting arrested at 15 for breaking beer bottles on the steps of the courthouse.
How stupid do you get?
Depends on who you hang out with.

But that wasn't enough, so next, I visited a house known for drugs trafficking.
Got arrested in a drug bust.
How did all this happen?

Just got around the wrong people.
It can and does happen to so many good kids out there.
I was one of the lucky ones who got through it.

Those, of course, are extreme cases of a child gone wrong, and it doesn't have to be that way, but still, you do what your friends do.

Look closely at those you hang out with and make a decision. Are these people where I want to be, are they headed where I want to go? If not, perhaps it is time for a new group.

As an adult when you look at who you hang out with, you have to ask the same questions.
Some things never change.

If you find you are the top person in your group, you need to change groups.
If you are the one everyone learns from, you need to find a new group you can learn from.
If you are on the throne giving the orders, find a new group. You are no longer challenged nor learning.
You are in the number one problem with success called – comfortable.

Look at your five best friends (excluding family, you cannot do anything about them).

Here is what you will usually learn about them:
- They usually live in similarly priced houses.
- Make within $3000-$5000 a year of what you do.
- Drive similar value cars.
- Go on similar vacations.
- Do the same things on weekends.

- Have similar dreams and aspirations.

Now, don't get me wrong. Friends are very important to you and to your success.
But if you have a vision, you need to be around others who have a vision and want more.
If you have a dream, you need to be able to share it and get encouragement about it.

If you want to do so much more than those you hang out with, you need to find people who are looking for the same things that you are.
Fired up and ready to roll!

It is a plain and simple fact that if you want to make a million dollars a year, then hanging out with those who make 50K is not going to get you there. Just a plain and simple fact.

You need to hang out with people who are where you want to be.

You need to change your friends.
You need to hang out with people who dream the way you do, or even bigger.

People who have vision.
People who follow what they want.
Who are going for it.
Who are willing to take the chance, risk it all, and go for the gold.

People who are driving forward, just like you.
People who are where you want to be or doing all they can to get there.

If you are driven to make money and build a business and grow your value, then start hanging out with people who are doing it. People who want it as bad as you do.

I heard a great line the other day on an audio from Grant Cardone,

"most successful entrepreneurs bowl about 100… how come? Because they are not bowling on Tuesday night every week. They are building their business."

If you have a dream, then you need to go out and find others who are like you and start to hang out with them. It is how you will get your energy going in the right direction. Otherwise, you will get so busy with day to day tasks that you will never move forward.

If you are the smartest, sharpest, the best of those you hang out with.
If you are the "TOP DOG."
The person who is doing it all.
Guess what?

You need to find a new group.

If you are not driven by yourself and encouraged by those around you.

Then You are not learning.
You are not growing.

You are not on your way to making the dreams and vision you have into a reality.
Time to get off the train you are on and get on a new one.
Time to put your ladder against a different building.

Chapter 2 Exercises

Right now I want you to stop and take a moment. Let us together work this simple exercise and see what we learn about doing so much better.

1/   Make a list of the people you hand out with the most these days.
      1/
      2/
      3/
      4/
      5/

2/   Make a list of the people you want to be like and should hang out with tomorrow. (OK to include celebrities) You know the people, the ones you admire and have great respect for. Do not limit your vision here or anywhere.
      1/
      2/
      3/
      4/
      5/
      6/
      7/
      8/
      9/
      10/

      You can list as many as you can think of.

3/   Now go and make the changes.

Move forward with new people who are going where you want to be.
Places where you could meet these people include:
Attend a conference where people who you want to be like are speaking.
Attend a local meet-up group for entrepreneurs.
Join a mastermind with other entrepreneurs.

One final word of advice.
Many of you may have your own story of hanging out with the wrong people.
I remember hanging out with the wrong people.
Every day we would hang out doing nothing and talked about what we couldn't do.
How it was someone else's fault for all our problems and all the problems in the world.
How it was not really worth trying that hard.
What for?

A group of people who thought nothing could be done.
A group of people who thought they could do nothing.

Then what happened?
See the next chapter for the answer to that question.

Whatever you do, make sure that you take this chapter seriously.
It may be one of the most important chapters in the book.
Look at who you hang out with and make the changes you need to.
I know at this point it might seem very hard, but you can do it.
If you really are chasing that dream, then you have to do all the things you need to in order to get there.

Chapter 3

The Few, The Proud, The Marines. USMC

"Some people spend an entire lifetime wondering if they made a difference in the world. But the Marines don't have that problem."

Ronald Reagan

I was going through life thinking negatively and like there was nothing that could be done about it.

Then what happened next?
Then one day I woke up and I was in Paris Island, SC. Home to USMC boot camp.
I was in the Marines.
I wasn't yet a Marine, but I was in the Marines.

As we pulled into Paris Island on that dark night, the tone, the air, the feeling changed. We were in another world. Hell, perhaps? When that sergeant came on the bus and said, get you A**es off this bus, now. Well, at that point we knew it… we were definitely in another world.

If you don't know, Paris Island is an island surrounded by swamp and who knows what else. It's almost impossible to get off of unless you go out the front gate. A few have tried, and some were never heard from again. So, I was here for a while.

The crazy thing was the transformation. I was transformed, transported, from an environment where we believed we could do nothing to an environment where we knew there was nothing we could not do.

It is a total mindset change.
When you change your thinking, you can then change anything.

This is not a USMC recruiting book.
But I can tell you it worked for me and I want to share the attitude adjustment that happened to me, more than anything else.
The attitude of success.

Let me just take a moment and reinforce that thought with you.
> From an attitude that said, "I can't do anything."
> To an attitude that says, "There is nothing I cannot do."
> WOW!
> That simple phrase says it all.

The Few, The Proud, The Marines

Why are the Marines considered the top branch of the service? (I know I will take a little flack on this)

Why are there less than a quarter million marines at a time, active and reserves?

I do not claim to know that total answer, but I can tell you that attitude is key.
The attitude that nothing is impossible and that there is nothing I cannot do has a great deal to do with it.

When I went into the Marine Corps, I was a long-haired 17-year-old kid, out of shape, undisciplined and usually in trouble. I had a terrible attitude. I was going nowhere.

When I came out 13 weeks later, my entire life had changed.
I was now an 18-year-old man.
In the best shape of my life.
Totally disciplined
And ready to do anything I needed to with a firm belief there was nothing I could not do.

Why?
The major change was that of my attitude.
I now had an attitude that I said there was nothing I could not do.
A far cry from where I had been only 3 months earlier.

Amazing stuff, that USMC boot camp.
But the interesting thing you might not know is that Marine Corps training is much more mental than physical.

I was really out of shape and yet I learned how to do all the physical stuff. I even learned to do much of it very well.
But the mental journey was the one that changed my life.
The mental journey was the hardest thing in my life up to that point.

It is simply amazing when you see this put into action.
The attitude that no matter what the barrier is, it cannot stop me.
That changes your whole perspective.

And that, above all, is what I hope you will take from this book.

Nothing can stop you if you believe it.

If you have the attitude that you can do it.
You will be amazing.

I went from an environment where everything is hard and seemingly impossible.
The unfortunate environment that so many people live in today.

To an environment where there is nothing that you cannot do.
WOW!

Do you think this will help you to look at life differently?
Look at life as a positive instead of negative.
What happens to you when you believe there is nothing you cannot do?

Plain and simply put:
You become amazing and unstoppable when it comes to success.
Nothing can stop you.
That is now your attitude.

I remember how it felt to all of a sudden be surrounded by people who could do anything.

At first, you are totally stopped in your tracks. You want to say, "this cannot be."
But then you get sucked in and you go with it and your whole world changes.

A key part of USMC training is putting you through intense training that builds your confidence.

One of the toughest, yet as you do it, the greatest training opportunities they have is called, The Confidence Course. True to its name, it helps you to build up some amazing confidence.

One of the most challenging encounters you face, yet once you get it, one of the most fun pieces, is called "the slide for life."

This exercise begins with a high tower which has cables coming down from the top, over a pond of water to the shore on the other side. It is perhaps 25 yards.

Your objective, fully dressed for battle, with a full pack, is to climb to the top of the tower, get situated on the cable and slide to the bottom while staying on top of the cable. Seems simple enough, right?

The problem is that if you flip, you have to let go and drop down into the muddy water and start all over again. Once you flip, there is no way to get back on top.

The same thing happens if you lose your balance and end up hanging by your arms. It's time to let go and drop into the muddy water.

The course is built to give you confidence in making it happen.

But even more in the entire team of Marines, you are working with to make it happen. Everyone has to make it to the bottom.

You see, it is not just about you successfully making it through the course; it is about everyone on your team making it.

It took a while, I personally was hanging and flipping a few times, but I did it. we all did it.

Remember, our attitude was simple, there is nothing we could not do so certainly this was not going to stop us.

A key factor to remember is that when you are building yourself, your confidence, your skills, it is always good to look around and asked the questions: "Who else can I help with this? Who else is struggling with this? How can I help them?"

Chapter 3 exercises

To get discipline is to get that magic ingredient that can really change your life.
What is one thing that has been standing in your way?
Something you know you can do, but you are not doing it.
Something perhaps you are not sure you can do, and that is why it is not getting done.

Lose x pounds.
Exercise 3 times a week.
Stop something
Start something.

Pick one thing.
Commit to working it tomorrow, no excuses nothing in your way.
Then make that commitment every day, one day at a time.
Watch what happens.

Chapter 4

You Are Amazing

"We are what we believe we are!"

C.S. Lewis

YOU ARE Amazing!

You Are Amazing.
Just take a look at you.

God built you to be an amazing machine, totally synchronized.
Integrated.
Built for maximum output.
With more storage space in your brain and more processing power than any known computer in a head that measures on average less than the size of a basketball.
You are different from everyone else around you.
You might have some of the same things, but you are you.

You have been put here for your own purpose, your own mission.

And once you learn there is nothing you can't do, you will be even more amazing.

Don't let anyone ever tell you anything different.

As for me, I jump out of bed every morning and I say –

I am Amazing.

But understand that I don't do that to brag or because I am convinced or conceited.

I do it because I, like each of your reading this book, was made with that power, energy, and gift to do anything we want.

The only reason you are not doing it is that you are holding yourself back.

Once you remove that and once you stop holding yourself back, you too will see that you are

AMAZING.

Amazing is defined as - causing great surprise or wonder; astonishing.

Are you ready?

Here are some other words for amazing:
astonishing,
astounding,
fabulous,
fantastic,
fantastical,
incredible,
marvelous,
miraculous,
phenomenal,
prodigious,
stupendous,
unbelievable,
wonderful,
wondrous.

Whatever word you want to use, just pick one.
Now tomorrow and every day going forward, get up in the morning and know that you really are amazing.
Jump out of your bed and say it –

I am Amazing.

Some may think you are a bit crazy, but aren't we all when we are totally focused on making it happen in our lives?

With that attitude, you are on your way to doing anything you want to do.
Accomplishing anything you want.
You're amazing.

Chapter 4 Exercises.

This chapter exercise is really simple.
Start believing by doing.
Get up tomorrow morning and say it.
Even if you only say it to yourself.

I am amazing.
I am amazing.

Every morning
Watch how that smile comes to your face and you start the day so much more positive.
You will be smiling long before you even say it.
Get ready and watch what happens in your life.

Once you get it, once you believe it – you will be amazing.

I AM Amazing.

Do it.

<u>As Psychotherapist and great speaker Marisa Peer makes, "that you believe what you tell yourself FAR MORE than what other people tell you. That's why people often turn away from compliments - they simply don't believe it of themselves.</u>

<u>You are amazing.</u>
<u>Believe it and do it.</u>

Chapter 5

Stop Limiting Yourself

> I am the greatest.
> I said that even before I knew I was.
> Don't tell me I can't do something.
> Don't tell me it is impossible.
> Don't tell me I'm not the greatest.
> I am the double greatest.
>   Muhammad Ali

As I said earlier, we are our greatest enemy or our greatest supporter when it comes to success.

Once you decide to stop letting things get in your way, you are almost there.

The mental game is a key piece of what makes us successful.

You have to believe inside your head that you can do anything and that nothing is going to stop you. You must know this long before you can ever make it happen in the real world.

Think back to a time when you had something on your mind that you really wanted to accomplish, and you just went for it.

When you think about it, you know you had a vision of what it was going to be like to get there, long before you ever got there, didn't you? You felt it. You smelled it. You were there. You let it go through your mind again and again.

I can remember moving up to the big leagues in youth baseball, the 13-year-old division.   That huge field, fast pitchers, long baselines, and an outfield that went on forever, thinking about getting my first hit. I could see it. I could feel it. I knew I could do it. I felt it. I dreamed about it.

Then the day came, I hit the ball and it was just like the vision I had, only better. Running to first base, safe. Wow!

You see our mind really is that driver that can either help us to make it or totally shut us down.

You know that old story – the angel on one shoulder and the devil on the other.
    The fighting back and forth
        You can do it, don't worry about what your mama said.
        No, you can't do that, it is bad.

People make fun of it, but it is a real thing that goes on in our mind.
    Your mind controls your actions.

You do what you believe you can.
If you don't believe it, you are never going to do it.

Classic story. Everyone wakes up in the middle of the night and start thinking about all these things that could happen to you, but usually, they never do happen. You start going down all these roads. What if, what if, what if.

Clear out your mind.
Focus it on what you want in life.
Make the image bigger than life.
Remember how you used to dream when you were younger.
If you can get that energy going, there is nothing that is going to stop you.

You have to learn to condition your mind to remove all the junk.
You have to get your attitude to that level that will never give up.

Fear will hold you back if you let it.
But once you overcome it, nothing will stop you.

Chapter 5 Exercises:

Ok, you may have heard me talk about it.
You have read the book.
Now it is your turn.

Go to a place you love.
Allocate 2 hours of time.
Get comfortable
Start thinking about what you want and what has held you back from making it happen in your life.

No paper
No computer, phone or iPad.
Just let it roll in your mind.
Once you have it, you will never forget it.

After the time
Go home
Write it all down
You are now on your way.
You have the base, now all you have to do is build the plan and make it happen.
We are going to help you get there.

Chapter 6

Never Put a limit on Your Dreams

Christopher Reeve. "So many of our dreams at first seem impossible, then they seem improbable, and then, when we summon the will, they soon become inevitable."
                                        Christopher Reeve.

  Please take a moment and say it again and let it really sink in.

Never Put a limit on Your Dreams

Remember that those dreams are your future.
They are where you want to go.
They are your rocket fuel to get there.
Guard them and let them drive you forward.
Nothing is going to stop you once you believe.

Most of you have watched the Olympics, I imagine?
You've watched those athletics give it all.
They are amazing, aren't they?

But then so are you.

Most of these athletes have spent the majority of their life, including most of their childhood, getting ready to win the gold medal.

They have been training early in the morning, late at night, when they had extra time and even when they did not have the time, they made it happen.

They are on a schedule.
It is the only way they get it done.
They are totally disciplined and working just for that piece of gold.

Just for that gold medal.
Just for that opportunity to know they are the best in the world.

That is called dedication.
That is what you are going to develop as you read this book and do the exercises and go for what you really want in life.

For those of you out there who love soccer as I do.
Just look at the dedication of the world cup soccer player.
Totally dedicated to the game.
It is their life.

In small nations, we see great power in the sport.
We see great players.
We see them going for it all.

If soccer is not your game, what about American Football?
How about those Eagles?

If you live in the Philadelphia area, I bet most of you are Eagles fans, I am not among them.
(Love my Cowboys, don't be a hater)

Yet I still loved the victory of the Philadelphia Eagles.
Finally, in 2018, they won the Superbowl.

Their fans all saw the Eagles win the Superbowl.
After all those years of losing and getting beaten and listening to all the crap.
You see, that is what dreams are made of.
Dreams make things happen.

The question to each of you out there is – what is your dream?
What is it that you want to accomplish?
Where is it that you want to Go?
Don't limit it.

Not the dream someone else has for you.
Not where you think you should go.

What is your dream?

Chapter 6 Exercises

What is your dream?
Take some time right now and write it down right here in the book.
What is your dream?

Be honest.
Make sure it is your dream.
Make sure it is what you want.

Forget what others say or have said.
Forget what the world thinks.

What is your dream?
This is what is going to drive you as you move forward.

Don't give it up.
Don't compromise on it.
Don't settle for anything less.

Let this dream drive you forward.
Go for it.

Chapter 7

Stretch Yourself

"When you stretch your mind, you stretch the world around you."
Gustavo Razzetti

Now that you have figured out where it is you want to go, I want you to stretch, where ever that is, and find out how to go even further.

Begin by really asking yourself, "Is that enough? Or do I really want much more than that? Am I holding myself back?"

Go for the goal that you really want. But remember, you have to believe it in your mind first.

Then Maximize it
Push yourself even further.
I want you to go for the gold and settle for nothing less.
In your mind, make it happen.
See it happening.
Feel it.

We have a tendency to underestimate what we can really do.

I only think I can sell 500K next year when you know you already have 400K in the bucket, but you want to be safe. Instead, you should be going for the 800k – 1000k and even more.

Stretching means to stop playing it safe and go for it.
That might be a hard, new step for many of you, yet you can do it.

Many of you might be of the mindset where you feel that you always have to exceed your goals so you set them to a level that you know you can make. I see this all the time. It is good to exceed your goals, but if your goal is 100 units and you know you can do 200, why isn't your goal 250?

Setting reachable goals is all well and good and it makes you feel great, but it never gets you to where you could potentially be. Go for the impossible and end up so much further down the road. Shoot for the stars and you might end up on Mars.
Shoot for Mars and you will end up on the moon.
Set those goals higher.

As one of my favorite motivational people says – "you got to 10x it." Grant Cardone

Let's look at an example to better clarify this process.

You make 50k this year – you are young, new to the business, and you figure that was a good year.

Now as you plan next year, you set a goal of 10% gain, 55k.
You know you can do it if you just work a bit harder.

Also, at the end of the year, you make 58k and you have exceeded your goal and you feel great. Next year over 60.

Your friend, however, likes to set extreme goals because she knows it makes her stretch to levels way beyond what she thinks she can do. It also makes her so much more successful.

She too made 50K this year – a good year, just like you.
But instead of 10% gain for next year like you, she is going for 100% gain – to 100K

She busts her tail all year, everyone keeps telling her that in the world today her goal seems like an impossible one. Nonetheless, it drives her.

You see, goals drive you, but goals that are really hard, tough, and far out there? They make you maximize your ability, skills, drive and everything else you have.

At the end of the year, she is at 85K, short of her goal, but way beyond where you ended up.

If she had set her goal at 55K, she never would have made the 85K because she just would not have worked with the same energy, drive, and ambition.

You see, the further the target, the harder you have to work in your mind to make it real. The harder you work in your mind, the harder you work in life.

Set those goals high and it will make you stretch.

You can do so much more.

Chapter 7 Exercises

Now it is your turn to make this happen for you.
Are you ready?
Are you pumped up?
Are you excited?
Remember, never forget that you are amazing!
Did you get up this morning, jump out of bed and say, "I am Amazing?"

First, I want you to set your goals just like you normally would for the next year.
Now, look at them.
Feel them.
Make them part of you.

Now say to yourself, "what if."
>   What if I raised that goal by 10%?
>   What if I raised it by 25%?
>   What if I raised it by 50%, 100%, or 200%?

Pick one and go for it; just make sure it is above what you think you can do.
If you really want to test this for yourself, then I recommend going for no less than 50%.
Do it and watch what happens.

Chapter 8

Remove Your Limits

"Don't limit yourself. Many people limit themselves to what they think they can do. You can go as far as your mind lets you. What you believe, remember, you can achieve."
                                    Mary Kay Ash

    You can do so much more – but you have to remove those limits that you have placed on yourself.

When I was working in the tradeshow industry, I use to spend a great deal of time on the west coast of the US in California, working with my teams and partners.
We could be anywhere from San Francisco to San Diego or any place in between, or even out to Las Vegas.

Now if you have worked and driven in California or on the west coast, you have to be familiar with the road the I-5.

It's very similar to the east coast route 95 except I think it has at least twice as many lanes on it.

It runs from above Seattle down to San Diego.

One day I was with one of my west coast partners, in his Corvette, with me driving.
Huge engine, 6 speed, living the dream.

Just cruising down the I-5 and loving it.
I pop the car into 4th gear and it screams.
When I look down at the speedometer, we are doing about 110 miles per hour – no limits.

Now I am not here to encourage you to speed.
But what I am trying to teach you is that when you take the limits off, you will be amazed at what you can do and where you can go and just like in the Corvette – fast.

Just take a moment and think about your life.
Think about what you can do and where you could go if you took the limits off and just went for the gold.

Get out a piece of paper or use your electronic device to capture what you think about when you do this.

Wow!
What if I did that?

Think about it and think about what it is that is limiting your life from doing it? What is holding you back from what you really want to do?

Why are you not going for it?
What do you have to do to make it happen?

Don't fall into using the same excuses everyone else does.
    I am not lucky.
    They had help.

They had it made.
I have more responsibility
I don't have that much time; I have a family.

You have other things that are important in your life and important to your success, but that should not be holding you back, you just need to figure out how to make it work.

Also remember the key point to success. Success is not excelling at one thing that costs you everything else in your life – success is having it all. Business, family, health, faith.

My greatest success in life is my 3 very successful children. All the rest are important and good, but these children are at the top.

Yet, I still am successful in business and doing well.
My health is great.
My marriage is outstanding.
Plus, my faith has never been stronger.

Why?
Because I, like you, have learned how to go for what I want.

You can do anything you want.

Take a moment and let's go back and remember when you were 6 and anything was possible.
What is different now?
Everything is still possible, that has not changed.
What has changed is your mind – you have changed.
You have limited your thinking.

But the good news is that you can get it back.
You cannot go back there, but you can get the mindset.

What is it that you think is out of your limits?
Make a list.
Write it down.

Then remember this, it is only out of your limit if you think so.
If you mentally believe that, it will be.

Henry Ford said it many years ago, "If you think you can, you can. If you think you can't, you can't. Either way, you are correct."

How can you make your life work the way you dreamed it could be?
That is the answer you are looking for.
That is why you are still reading this book.
You want it all.

Now go out and get it.

Chapter 8 Exercises

Let's define those things that seem to be holding you back.

Make a list right now.
You know what you really want.
Write it down.

Now answer these questions for each thing you really want:
1/   What is holding you back from getting it?
2/   What can you do about it?
3/   How important is it?

You now have your working document to make this happen in your life.

Mindstorm your answer
(Check out my video to learn about mindstorming)

Mind Storming - Drilling for real gold

https://youtu.be/Q2IZ1arWm3o

Define 20 things you can do about it.
Don't judge.
Just make the list.

Then go back and pick the best 3 things you could do to make it happen

You will be amazed.

Here's a similar exercise that's incredibly powerful from my friend, professional speaker Elaine Starling:

Think of something you want to accomplish - a goal.

On a scale of 1 - 10 where 1 is you haven't started yet and 10 is you've completed your goal to your full satisfaction, where are you?
What number pops into your head?
Maybe you picked a 3.
Whatever number you think first, it's the right number for you right now.
Why did you pick such a high number?

Asking this question is really powerful because it forces you to look at everything you've done so far on your goal.

Just setting the goal requires you to research your current situation, evaluate your competition, consider your skills, abilities, and resources, and mentally map out a plan of action.

Take 2 minutes to write down something you could do in one hour that would move you closer to your goal.
Write down as many things as you can think of, each one taking no more than one hour to do. Break big projects down into one hour steps.

Now take 2 minutes to review and prioritize your list. What would you do first? What comes next?

Do the first thing on your list immediately.

If you have the time, tackle the next one on your list.

You'll feel momentum build and your enthusiasm grow as you realize how much progress you've already made!

Chapter 9

Opinions are like? - Everyone has one, and they all stink.

"If someone isn't what others want them to be, the others become angry. Everyone seems to have a clear idea of how other people should lead their lives, but none about his or her own."

Paulo Coelho

You have to be willing to live without the opinion of others, to find your true self and unlock your full capabilities. Do you get that?

This is one of the biggest roadblocks you can encounter, and it can stop you cold in your
steps.

Our human nature makes us all want to be accepted, it is part of our makeup, and we can do
Little about it, well, maybe.

Don't you ever believe this!

As we can actually do a great deal about it, but we have to do something to get started.

No one wants to become totally isolated from the world. So, you will encounter the
opinions of others, and that's just life.

However, please think about what you are doing when it comes to the opinions of others.

First, understand that someone being negative will take you there if you let them.
They want company.

Here is a sad and dangerous truth.
Hanging out with people who are negative, will make your negative.
There is no other direction.

If you take nothing else from this book, please surround yourself with positive people.

If you do nothing else, that alone will take you down a whole new road.

As I said initially, you are the average of the five people you hang out with the most.

You need to change your group.
It would be best if you hung out with people who are going to pump you up and make you rock.

People who want what you want.
People with your attitude.
People who are where you want to be.
People who are going to the same place as you.

Just think about how great you feel when you get that positive
 experience.
Surrounded by others who are where you want to be, pumped
 up and pumping you up.

You get positive, energy building feedback from others.
Think about how it makes you feel.
How it helps you to believe.

Find some new people to hang out with and get rocking.

Chapter 9 Exercise.

Take some time to define these as they relate to YOU!

Who are the people you spend the most time with right now?
Write their names down here.
Remember family is family, there is nothing you can do to
change them, except love them and try to teach them
what I am trying to teach you.

Checkmark the negative ones?
Do you see them ever changing? Really?

If not, or you are unsure, get them off your real hang out
people and find a new group and new
friends.

If you want to be great, you have to hang out with people like
you or act how you want to be.

You can take that one to the bank.

Note: this is not an easy thing to do, so don't think it is, but
negativity can utterly destroy you. Do not let it.

Section 2 – The Three Keys to Success

"When a man really finds himself, at the top of the ladder of success, he is never alone because no man can climb to genuine success without taking others along with him."

                                                            Napoleon Hill

Listen to daily tip on this from Coach Manny Nowak.
https://youtu.be/FgU2kz4I8CQ

Now that I have you pumped up, and you're ready to go, what can you do to make all we have spoken about in section one of the book, actually happen in your life?

This process all started with just a motivational piece that got you pumped up.

However, I learned that was not enough to actually make it happen in your life.

If you want to change, you have to have a way to make it happen.

So many people think they want to do it, but they never find the way, then they give up and continue to do what they have been doing.

You are not part of that group – you and the five people you will hang out with the most – are rocking.

To make it happen, you have to have the three things we will talk about in the rest of this book.

They are a vision, a written plan and taking action.

So now that you are pumped up let's go and make it happen. Also, if you need more pumping up right now, stop and watch this video.
The Successful Will Never Tell You, "You Can't. Day 116

https://youtu.be/bz2LXdOVvnk

Chapter 10

Vision

Vision without action is daydreaming
Action without vision is a nightmare
Vision with action is beautiful reality.
                From the Book, Beside Still Water.

Vision is the first sign you will see on the road to success.

It is big, it is bold, and it gets your attention.

Vision!

Right now, close your eyes(unless you are driving or doing something that needs your attention) and just think about what you really want in life. Don't rush. Take your time doing this, just let your mind wander into the future.

Where are you?

What does it look like?
What does it feel like?

Do this for a bit, then when you stop, write down everything you think is important. Then keep this for the future.

Now ask yourself this question - What do you really want in life?

When I randomly asked people this question, they usually don't have an answer.

They know they are not where we want to be.
But because they don't know where they really want to be, they will never get there.
Without a destination, you are just wondering about.

When I ask people, "what is your vision for your life?"
They give me this look.
The same one that might just be on your face right now.

Starting there is OK.
Don't feel like there is nowhere to go.
That is why you are reading this book.
You want to know what it is.

So, stop right here and do me a favor, take out a piece of paper (yes paper and pen) and write down what your vision for your life is. If you did the exercise above, then use those notes and put it together. If you did the exercise earlier in the book, use that information as well.

Don't short change this, write it down.
Take your time.
Give it some thought.

I have worked with teams and with individual people, and sometimes it takes days of going back again and again until we have it nailed down.
This is your foundation.
This is your base.
Take your time and make sure it is what you really want.

If you don't really have one, then write it down," I really don't have one."
We have to start some place.
Someone taught me years ago that when I hit a writer's block where I am just empty to write it down: I can't think of anything. Amazing things happen.

If you don't have an answer, don't feel like you are the only person in the world without an answer. You are not.
Actually, if you have a vision, you are among the minority of people.

It is our natural tendency to think – well everyone else has one, why don't I?
Wrong, most people do not have a vision
And even of those that do, few have it written down.

If you hit a roadblock here, stop, don't feel like you are the only one.

Remember that because of who you are, this will never stop you.

You are amazing!

Have you been getting up and doing that every morning?

If not, go back to early in the book.

You are unstoppable.
You are going through, over, under or around this roadblock, just hang in there and keep on going. This is where you need those five people around you who give you energy.

Most people don't have a written vision.
Further, most people have never shared their vision with anyone.

Some had a vision at one point in their lives and let someone disrupt it, blow it away, take it from them. It stopped them cold, but not you.

What I am asking you to do is go for it.
What I am asking you to do is to take off all the constraints.
Think, "where could you go in your life if you did not have anything holding you back?"
Think, "nothing is limiting you!

What is down that road that you could have?

Where can that road take you on the path to success?

Where do you want to be?
30 years from now? Write it down.

20 years from now? Write it down.

10 years from now? Write it down.

5 years from now? Write it down.

3 years from now? Write it down.

1 year from now? Write it down.

Who has ever asked you these questions in your life?
Have you ever taken the time to think about them?
Do it now.
Write the answers down.
This is going to change your life.

We as Americans are so short term focused.
Today, tomorrow maybe one more day out.

We spend more time planning our vacations, our weddings and our parties than we do planning our lives.

When you start to look at your life and let your mind go free.
Ask what you really want?
You will be amazed.

In our 90 days to Your Success training, this is the first question we ask you.
What do you really want in your life?

This may be the first time anyone has ever ask you that question.

Typically, when we look out so far, the first response we get is usually, I thought this was about 90 days? Why are we talking about 30 years from now?
I cannot even think 30 months from now.

Or I get this answer, are you kidding me, I might not even be here then. I am already x years old.

But you must look out that far.

This is one key that will make you different, and it will make you tremendously successful.

If you want to get to California and you live in New York, and you plan to drive,
You need a path and a plan to get there.

You can use a GPS.
We all have them these days, and they work great.
I love mine, and I use it all the time.

However, you still need to know exactly how to get to LA.
Plus, sometimes GPS can throw us off.
Like, just the other day I was looking for a printer to pick up an order we placed electronically, and the GPS said I was there, I was miles away.

Chapter 10 Exercises

Your assignment right here is fill in the blanks.
You don't have to be totally detailed.
You don't' have to write a book.
Neither are you are not locked into this for life or even for very long.

The key to remember.
If you want to have a fully paid for a mansion on the beach in Southern California 20 years from now, where do you have to be 10 years from now?

I love this stuff.
I know it works.
I wish I had of had much of it when I was younger, but who cares.
As long as we are still breathing, we should be going for it.

Go do it; it will really open your mind.

You need to give it a shot so you can see where you are and what you are thinking.
For each of these questions write your answer to these 3 points:

Goals by that time?
What does life look like?
What are you doing regularly?

30 Years from now?
Goals by that time?
What does life look like?

What are you doing regularly?

20 years from now?
Goals by that time?
What does life look like?
What are you doing regularly?

10 years from now?
Goals by that time?
What does life look like?
What are you doing regularly?

5 years from now?
Goals by that time?
What does life look like?
What are you doing regularly?

3 years from now?
Goals by that time?
What does life look like?
What are you doing regularly?

1 year from now
Goals by that time?
What does life look like?

What are you doing regularly?

Chapter 11

Road to Success

When I didn't like what I was doing, I still did it well while I was doing it, but I saw to it that I didn't do it any longer than I had to do it.
Napoleon Hill.

Watch Coach Manny Nowak Present this saying live.
https://youtu.be/SnoTvxAmn6c

Are you ready to be on that road and that path to success?
Make it part of you, go for it.
Write it down.
Really think about what it is that you want in life and move forward knowing that you can really have it.

If I observe young children, under 10 years old.
Many of you reading this may have them yourself.

These little ones, they have dreams for their lives.
They know what they want to be when they grow up, at least they know what they want to be today. Tomorrow it might be totally different, but that is because they are not afraid to change. They do not hesitate like you and me – they just go for it.

You can hear them saying:

I want to be a fireman.
I want to be the president

I was going to say, "I want to be an attorney," but does anyone really dream of that as a child?

I want to be a ship captain
I want to be a space captain – going to other planets, other universes.

I am going to be whatever I want.
If you ask them again next week, or next month or next year, they will probably give you a totally different answer, yet they will be solid in whatever they want to be.

The point is that they do have vision.
They dream big.
They know they want to do something big and they do not see anything stopping them.
The only limits they have are the ones we might create for them.

We so many times feel that we have to create a limit for them.
But we should not.
We have to let them go, grow, and be all they can.

I can remember myself as a child saying, "I am not going to work in a factory and deal with all you and my dad dealt with, I am going to own the factory. I am going to be Mr. Seabrook (the owner) not just a worker. I am going for the gold."

My mom also tried to bring me back to reality, as she called it. Still, I was having no part of that. Some of us just keep on dreaming.
Let nothing hold us back.

You see, somewhere in the cycle, probably around 14-16 we start putting these limiting factors on our children's lives, "for their own good."

We start to tell our children, well maybe that isn't possible for you!

That's garbage.
Anything is possible.
We as parents, as leaders and those people look up to, we need to stop this limiting thing for their good.
We need to encourage and push them to go even bigger.
We need to do it in all the places of our lives, home, family, friends, and work.

I spend a great deal of time on this with my own grandchildren.
Encouraging them to dream and to dream even bigger.
Take away the limits.

You can be president.
You can be the richest person in the world.
You can do anything.

Remember what I said about the 5 people you hang around with most?
How they need to be who you want to be.
They need to be motivated and inspired like you.
You will become like them, so they better be where you want to go.

So where do we go from here?

First, ask:
What is it you want?
Where is it you want to go?

Now, there is more you are going to need.

But first, let's do the assignment for this chapter.

Chapter 11 Assignment

Take out a blank sheet of paper and start writing down your vision.
It can be in pictures, words, numbers.
Just doodle – you are allowed.
See what you find hiding in that wonderful mind of yours.
You might just be amazed.

Chapter 12

Your Why

"Internal motivation is better than external motivation, and is a river of life within you that never runs dry, when you have a 'why', 'purpose' and 'dream'".
Chris T. Atkinson

The final thing you need is your why!
Why do you want this?
Why do you have this vision?
Why is this important to you?

Late at night when things are not going according to plan, what will keep you going?
The only thing that will keep you going is your Why!

When you talk about vision, you need a why.
Anyone can say "I am going to do this."
But how many actually get there?

Remember that making a lot of money is not really a vision; it is actually the result of a vision.
Why do you want to make a lot of money?

What do you need that money for?
What will you do with it?

Why you want to do something is that important.
Look at all the great people out there who wanted to change something and did.
They all had a vision.

You might be a young reader and not really remember who Bill Gates is, but he is the founder of Microsoft one of the largest companies in the world.
But Microsoft did not start there – Microsoft was once just a little start-up company just like you might own today.

But the difference is that Bill Gates had a vision.
Do any of you remember what that vision was?

Bill had a vision to put a computer in every home in America.
Do you think he made it?
He did.

When you look around your house, this might not seem a big deal, but if you looked around the average house 25 years ago, there were almost no computers.

When Bill said this was his vision, no one in small businesses had computers.
They cost a great amount of money at the time.

How could the average family ever have a computer?
But Bill had the vision that he was going to put a computer in every house.
Of course, now we see it has happened and it is no big deal.
But that was one heck of a vision.
You do not have to be that big, but you can be.
Just as Bill had no limits, neither do you.

When you write your book someday you can say, "I never really had a vision until I read about them in this book by Coach Manny Nowak, the rest is history, today we made my dream come true."

Steve Jobs the co-founder of Apple, also had a vision.
His vision was to put an Apple computer in every home.
Now you might say well that didn't happen.
Or did it?

Has he accomplished that task?
How many of you have an iPhone? iPod? iPad?
Amazing.

The key for you to remember here is that these where not multimillion-dollar people who worked for large corporations, had all the money in the world at their fingertips, and just played to make this happen.
Far from it.

They were really just like you and me.
Simple people.

However, they had a vision, they had a why, and they were not going to let anything stand in their way.

What I want you to take from this first section of the tools is that you can do anything.
That the only thing holding you back is yourself.
That you need to get out of your own way and go for the gold.
You need to stop hesitating.

Go back and ask the question of yourself.
What is your dream?
Why do you want it?
When are you going to get started?

Bill Gates and Steve Jobs were just like you and me.
What you need to remember is that you can do anything.

Remember also of those that do have vision – that is just the start of the process.
They might say, "Oh, I am going to do this or that".
But they don't do anything with it.
Which will take us to the second sign on the road to success – A Plan.

Chapter 12 Exercises

Now go back to what you put together at the end of the last chapter and read it.
Let your mind flow through it.
Read back through this chapter.
Then make any changes you feel that you need to.
You might not make any, but the key is I want you to remove the limits from your thinking.
I want you to think so much bigger, better, and stronger.

The only thing holding you back is you – get out of your own way.

Chapter 13

Plan

The Steve Job's Method:
Get People together.
Make a list of 10 things we should be doing next – get all in, cross off things that will not work.
Then get list to 10
Then cross off 7 of them
We can only do 3
Do them.

Not just a plan, it has to be a written plan.

The next question to all of you who have put a vision together is simply this,
Will you take that vision and before this week is done, put a plan together to make it happen?

How are you going to attain that vision?
What do you have to do to make it a reality?

As I am writing the original draft of this book, it is a couple of days after New Years Day 2019.

Every New Years, people have all kinds of visions and dreams.

Not sure if it is because of some help on New Year's Eve or what.

Next year I am going to?

Increase my sales to 10 million.
Stop smoking.
Spend more time with my family.
Build my own business and quit my job.

On and On and On.
Millions of these were just done a couple of days ago.

Now you know both you and I are positive people and on the road to success.
But this, unfortunately, is the truth.
I know because for so many years, I too was part of this group.

I call these people, "I was going to, but life got in the way."

Did you know that most of those visions, dreams, and wishes will be gone before the end of January and a great deal of the rest, will be going by March?

Only 2 percent of the people make it happen in their lives.
And as a reader of this book, you are part of that 2%.
Yes, you are.

That 2% that change the world.

So, the next thing you need on your path to success is a plan, you need a plan to make this happen in your life. This is not just a plan in your head, but a written plan.

I can remember the first meeting I was having with this 74-year-old business owner who was sharp as a whip and committed to growing his business.
I asked him, "do you have a plan?"
He said, "yep, got it all up here in my head."

And that, I told him, is why it had not yet happened.
Once I made him write it down, that is when things really started to change

Chapter 14

Goals

"The trouble with most of us is that we make happiness our goal instead of aiming at something higher, loftier and nobler."
        From the Book, The Secret of Happiness

For those who do not already know, I am a huge soccer fan.
I spent twenty years coaching the youth game and stop everything every 4 years to watch the World Cup.

In soccer, the objective is to **get a goal** but also to get more goals than the other team.

In life, we also have to go and get our goals.
You may have one or more goals for work.
One or more for play.
Many for your children.
Some goals for the other parts of your life.

Goals are destinations you want to get to, but they do not start your journey on the path to success.
They simply let you know where you want to go and when you get there.

As you look at your plan for the next 90 days, you have to ask yourself these questions, "what are my goals?"

Examples:

Is my goal to increase my sales by or to 1 million dollars?

Is my goal to get a promotion to a senior management position?

Is my goal to complete the invoicing project?

What is the goal?

Further, please don't limit this "90 Days to Your Success" process just to work.

Initially, I recommend only working with your business, but as you start to understand the process and see the great success you are achieving, you will see how easy it is to apply to other areas of your life.

It does not just have to be about work.
You can use all that I have helped you to develop in both your business and your personal life.

Some potential Targets to use this with.

Maybe you want to go back to school and get an advanced degree?

I receive great feedback this actually happened at a talk I gave late last year. One of the participants said, "I been thinking about this too long, I am going back to school."
I wish her much success.

Maybe you want to take your golf game to a new level.

Maybe you want to start a new business.

Just as we have been trying to teach you since the beginning of the book.
Don't put all those limits on yourself that others do.

We tend to think, "I can only make $2000 a year more next year.
I should be satisfied with that?"

Who said?

Why?

Well, that is higher than the most?
So what, go for the gold.
Remember that most people will go for being content. That does not do it for you. If you are still reading this book, then you want to go for the gold. Let nothing stop you.

Stop and remember this:

The Greatest enemy of success is contentment.

Chapter 14 Exercises

Write down your goals for the next year.
What do you want to accomplish over the next year in your life?
It doesn't matter if this is not the beginning of the year, go forward from here.

Then looking at those one-year goals, determine what your goals need to be over the next 90 days to move you toward them.

And again remember, write them down.

If you start here, you will be amazed at what happens in your life.

Once complete, you will know what your goals are for the next 90 days.

Chapter 15

Stretch/10X

"When you stretch your mind, you stretch the world around you."

                                              Gustavo Razzetti

A mentor of mine and someone I have a great deal of respect for is Grant Cardone.
If you have ever seen him in action, you would think I was a calm person. Grant is a Wildman, and he has had enormous success with his 10X process. I am a huge fan, and I love it.

He always tells us we need to take our goals and we need to 10x them.

But what does that mean?

To put it simply, we need to take each of our goals and then multiple by 10. If our goals are to get a $2000 raise, forget that, times it by 10 and make it $20,000.

If you want to increase your sales by $100,000, 10x it and make it a million dollars.
If you want to bring in 10 new customers, 10x it and shoot for 100.

Here is the thinking behind this and why you really need to use it.
If you shot for 100, you might get there or close, and that will be good. You might even make 120 and feel on top of the world. You have crushed your goal.

But if you 10x it to 1000.
You might only hit 575, but that is a whole lot more than 120? The higher you set your expectations, the higher your results. It really does work that way.

Our expectations are what we accomplish.

Expect to make $100 for the job, and that is what you make.
Expect to make $1000 for the job, and that is what you make.

Let me accomplish way beyond my thinking.
Remember what I have told you so far in this book, if you can see it in your mind you can make it happen.

And let no one else stop you.

That is why we call this; the successful will never tell you that you can't.
Do you get it now?

If you are hanging around with people who are very successful, they will encourage you; they will push you, they will help you to make it happen.

If you are hanging around the wrong people, you will never get there.

Chapter 15 Exercises

Are you ready to 10x your stuff?
You have to really feel good about this.
You have to really get pumped up.

If you are, then go back and 10x those goals from the last chapter.

If you don't feel that strong yet, write it down anyway. Look at it every day and say, "I can DO THIS!!!" You'll feel it eventually..

You will feel better at 10x, but the stretch is important. So really, any stretch will help you here.

Chapter 16
Tasks

Every block of stone has a statue inside it and it is the task of the sculptor to discover it.
                                        Michelangelo

You will need to develop tasks to accompany your goals: one or many for each goal.

Tasks are those things that make goals happen.
They are the things that so many people are missing when they commit to a goal. Then they wonder why they did not accomplish their goals.

As you look at your plan for the next 90 days, you have to ask yourself, how am I going to make these goals happen?

In other words, what should I do to accomplish these goals?

If you are familiar with project management, then you know about breaking things into smaller manageable units, this is the same process.
You can think of the goal as your project, and the tasks as the road that will get you there.
The things you need to do to make this project happen.

How complex or detail, depends on how complex and detail the goal is and how you work best.
When it comes to actual execution of the plan, you may break them down into even small units.

This is one of the pluses of looking at stuff 90 days at a time. It will allow you to get your hands around the tasks so much easier because the goals are shorter. The tasks happen so much quicker and are usually much smaller.

Even if the overall goals go beyond 90 days, what do you have to do in the next 90 days to meet the goal?

Getting the tasks right will keep you from becoming like so many people out there who talk about it but never do it.

Many people shoot off their mouth talking about, "I am going back to school" and "I am going to get an MBA." Then you see then three years later, and they say – "I am going back to school" and "I am going to get an MBA."

The tasks are the steps you need to make the goal real.

For example, if your goal is to go back to school and get an MBA, then what do you need to do to make that happen?

     1/   When? Are you going to start this?

     2/   Where are you going? Find three schools you want to attend.
     3/   How? Apply for acceptance
     4/   Pay? Secure the funds to pay for it.
     5/   Get accepted
     6/   Decide which school and when.

This is just a start, but you get the idea.

These are the tasks and executing these tasks is what makes the goal happen.

Not defining and thus not executing tasks is one of the big reasons people do not get things done. They simple fail to take time to understand the tasks that need to be done to make things happen

Important:
These tasks just like the goals must be written down.
If you do not write them down, then it will not happen.
Period.
You cannot do this in your head.
Trust me.
Many have tried.
It does not happen that way.

I have great fun listening to entrepreneurs who always tell me, "it is all in my head." I got it, Manny.
Then I would have to tell them, nope, it doesn't work, you have to write it down.
But Manny?

Chapter 16 Tasks

Now we get to the meat of the process.
For each of your 90-day goals, I want you to write down what you will do over that next 90 days to make this happen in your life. What are the tasks.
Don't go too crazy.
Anything you write here is a step in the right direction and will take you so much closer to making this happen in your life.

Do not hesitate here.

Example:
The goal is to sell 250 copies of my book.

Tasks:
Run three weeks of Facebook advertising at $10 a day.
Speak to three groups at the local college.
Attend two networking events and push the book.
Email my list every two weeks about the book.

You get the idea.
Real things to do to make this goal happen.

Now it is your turn.
Do it.

Chapter 17

Measurements.

"Subjectivity measures nothing consistently."
                                    Toba Beta

Few people like to be measured.
But, if you are not being measured, then how do you know you are moving forward?

How can you tell if you are on target?

Without measurement, it is like playing sports without keeping score .How much fun is that?
How can you tell where the game stands?

How do you know you are doing the things you set out to do unless you are measuring?

Not just do you need tasks to move forward on your goals, you also need measurements.
Measurements tell you two things.

1/   Either you are doing it, or you are not doing it.
2/   If you are not doing it, then you need to figure out what you need to do to make it happen for you.

Example: You want to bring in 100 new clients.

That means you need to identify 1,000 qualified prospects. You need to reach out to 10,000 companies to identify 1,000 prospects and convert them to 100 new clients.

Next you need to figure the answer to these questions:
    How many dials/day?
    How many voicemail messages/day?
    How many live calls/day?
    How many companies converted to prospects - or eliminated - per day?
Identify the numbers that matter - that allow you to complete or exceed your goal.

Chapter 17 Exercise

For each goal, you have set up the measurements.

You can also set these up for the tasks if they can be measured beyond just bring done or not done.

But make sure you set a measurement for each goal.
Then track that measurement as you go through the 90 days of process.

Keep your eye on it. Review your numbers first thing in the morning and last thing before you walk out the door at the end of the day.
Know at all times where you are.

Chapter 18

Accountability

"When it comes to privacy and accountability, people always demand the former for themselves and the latter for everyone else."
                                            David Brin

The other thing you will need to make all this work is accountability.
This is one thing that most people lack, and many people have a great fear of.
Tell someone you will hold them accountable for something and watch what happens to their face.

Here are 3 pieces you need to be accountable for.

1/   Are you hanging out with the right people?
        People who are pushing you forward in the right direction.
        People who make sure your ladder is against the right building.
        People who know you can do so much more and expect you to do it.

Expect you to start doing it - now.

2/ A Mentor
Everybody needs a mentor.
Somebody who has done what you want to do.
Somebody who is already making a great life it what you want to be.

One thing I can tell you, successful people will always help you if you ask.

Successful people are never too busy.
Successful people are not busy, they are productive.
Busy people are not necessarily successful, they are busy.
But you might have to be very persistent.

Don't be afraid to reach out.
Never be afraid to reach out and ask.
Ok, you can be afraid, but never let that stop you.
Fear sometimes creates new things in us we need to have.
The worse that could happen, you get a no.
Then you will have to ask again.

And go for the big ones.
Don't just settle for asking anyone.
I always like to start at the top
Go for Bill Gates and then work your way down.

Chances are very good that the higher you go, the better chance they will help you.

Very few people ask them because they are all afraid to, so ask.

But not you.

Go for it.

3/   A Coach

You need a coach.

Just like those in athletics need a coach so do people who want to be very successful in life. People like you.

You need someone who can make sure you are working the basics.

Remember, when you look at all athletes, the basics are what makes them great.

Look at all the great basketball stars and see how much time they spend on the line practicing foul shots. Because when they get to the line, then it just happens.

A coach cannot be your friend, they cannot be someone who is going to let you slide.
They have to be someone who can keep you on track. Who expects more of you than you can see. Who knows you want to make it happen and will help you get there.

When you have friends around you, and you are hanging out with the right people
When you know who you want to be like – mentor and are working with them.
When you have this person, coach, who keeps pushing you even further.

Just think of what you can do in your life when you add this to your mix?

Think about where you are right now, and where you really want to go.
Then ask yourself if doing this would really change things.
You see if you don't believe it, it will not happen.
If you do believe it, you are already 2/3 of the way there.

I want you to finish this book, not pumped up but I want you to finish the book ready to do something that will change your life, perhaps something you have been hesitating on. But more, then I want you to actually do it.

Chapter 18 Exercises

Take your mind and wipe it clean.
Have a clean board to start with.
Then just start putting this together.
What you could do.

1/   Who are those people you need to hang out with?

2/   Who are candidates to ask to be your mentor?

3/   Who could you hire to be your coach?

Chapter 19

90 days to your success.

The 90 days to success process is a new way of looking at your life.
> Manny Nowak

The method to the success we use to make all this happen is "90 Days to Your Success."
http://coachmanny.com/90-days-to-your-success/

This is the methodology we use to help make this happen in the lives of people.
It is wound around the concept of long-term goals and plans.
Short term action.

The question we start with is simple, what are you going to do in the next 90 days?

90 days is something most of us can get our hands around.
It is something we can feel.
Something we can touch.
Something we can do.

Today's world is moving so fast and you all reading this book are moving at such high speed. I encourage you to look at this tool and see if it might be something you could use.

It allows you to manage your life in 90-day increments.
It is amazing what we have been able to accomplish ourselves using this tool.
But even more what we have been able to help our clients to accomplish using this process.

The process starts 30 years from now, goes to 20 years, 10 years, 5 years, 3 years, 1 year and then 90 days.

It makes you think.
Then you take it even deeper. It takes you into 90 days, then one week and then one day.

You control your life.
You live a proactive life instead of a reactive life.

To learn more, go to
http://coachmanny.com/90-days-to-your-success/

After your first 90 days – your comment is
Wow!
Look what I just did.
We are creatures of gratification.
We love to know that we did something.
Doesn't it feel great when you accomplish something?
That is what this tool helps you to do - accomplish great things and then reflect on them and use that experience to do even more.

In 90 days you can look around, and you can say, we did all this in only 90 days – the sky is the limit, let's get those next 90 days rolling.

Section 3

Action is What makes it happen.

Do not be like the cat who wanted a fish but was afraid to get his paws wet.
                              William Shakespeare

This is the final piece of the puzzle, the final piece that will put all this together for you.

If you have a vision and you have a plan you are almost there. What you need now is to do something about it.

The simple fact is that many people have a vision, some might even have a very detail plan, but they do nothing about it.

They never execute.
There are some great visionaries in the world.
There are some great planners in the world.

But the ones who actually take action, they make it happen. The ones who have a vision, plan and then execute that plan, they are the extraordinary ones.

Just like you.

Take a look at all those entrepreneurs out there doing it.

If you are still reading this book, then you are one of those people.

In this final piece, we will examine some of these execution tools in more detail.

Chapter 20

Persistence

"I had learned, from years of experience with men, that when a man really desires a thing so deeply that he is willing to stake his entire future on a single turn of the wheel in order to get it, he is sure to win".
Thomas Edison - first meeting with Edwin Barnes

Persistence makes it happen.
Have you ever surfed?

If you have you understand the goal is to keep riding a bigger and bigger wave.
To make this happen, you have to have the persistence to keep going and conquer the current wave. Not just ride it but conquer it and move to the next level.

Whatever it is that you want to go for, if you build your mindset and say, "nothing is going to stop me, I am not going to let anything get in my way." Then if you are persistent in moving forward with a total determination to conquer it. It will happen.

What do you think you could do in your life if you had this attitude?
You could ride the wave you want to ride.

Let me share with an article with you on persistence.

Article:

Persistence creates success - plain and simple

How bad do you want it?

How much are you going to do to get there?

Are you going to be successful or are you going to quit? Remember, it is always easier to quit.

The wisdom of Napoleon Hill with a simple quote: "No man is ever whipped until he quits - in his own mind."

Have you quit in your own mind or will you keep going until you make it happen?

Today, let us examine these four steps for persistence by Napoleon Hill.

1/ A definite purpose backed by a burning desire for its fulfillment

2/ A definite plan, expressed in continuous action

3/ A mind closed tightly against all negative and discouraging influences, including negative suggestions of relatives, friends, and acquaintances

4/ A friendly alliance with one or more persons who will encourage one to follow through with both plans and purpose.

Let us examine this simply in terms of today's economic times.

1/ A definite purpose backed by a burning desire for its fulfillment

   Do you know what you are going after and are you totally committed to making it happen, or are you just talking about it? If you are selling a product or service, how much commitment do you have to make it work?

Are you just talking about it, or are you going to do it?

Shakespeare, that great writer, put it in simple terms:
"Assume a virtue if you have it not -
Look the part
Dress the part
Act the part
Be successful in your own thoughts first
It won't be long before you will be successful before the world as well"

Sales down?

Customers not buying?

How are you acting when you walk in?

How do you talk to them?

Are you showing success or failure?

They are watching you.

2/ A definite plan, expressed in continuous action

How many people do you know who talk about the plan they have -

in their minds? I have a plan, yes. But what are you doing

to make it happen?

You see, as Russell Conwell puts it, "Dream of future bigness,

but be ready to begin at once, no matter how small or

insignificant the beginning may appear to others"

Do something today and move you and your customers forward.

Now, today.

3/ A mind closed tightly against all negative and discouraging
    influences including negative suggestions of relatives,
    friends, and acquaintances

Now let's get the negative out of the process. We get so sucked
    up by that negative that we don't even know it is happening.
    Plus, as much as we hate to admit it, those closest to us are
    the worst carriers.

Close your mind to the negative; it is that simple.

You see Robert Collier in Acre of Diamonds puts it very simply:
"The difference between the successful man and the unsuccessful
one is not so much a matter of training or equipment. It is
not a question of opportunity or luck. It is just in the way
that each of them looks at things."

How are you looking at things today?

Positively or negatively.

You set the stage.

You direct the play.

You can either make it happen or watch it happen.

Which will you choose?

If you keep watching too long, soon you will be the spectator and someone else will have your job.

4/ A friendly alliance with one or more persons who will encourage one to follow through with both plan and purpose. Who has your back? Who is on your team to encourage you and keep you rolling? Who are you talking with to keep you accountable and on track?

Remember, if you need help with any of this, that is what we do best.
Schedule 15-30 minutes with me.
Link: **https://meetme.so/coachmannynowak**

Chapter 20 Exercises

Select one thing in your life you have wanted but have not achieved yet. Not a huge thing, just something simple. Now put together 3 things you can do to consistently be working it.

Then execute.

If you get there, great.
If not, add or change some things you are doing.
Then go at it again.
And again.
And do not stop until you have made it.
The feeling is unbelievable.

Once you master that one thing, you will be amazed.
Start simple.
Then add another.
Do the same thing.
Once mastered.
Another.

Now it becomes a habit, and you will be amazed at the results.

Chapter 21

Discipline

The secret of discipline is motivation, when a man is sufficiently motivated, discipline will take care of itself.

                                                Alexander Patterson

Let's go back to my time in the USMC.
Discipline is a skill you must learn to make it through USMC boot camp.

What is discipline?

According to the dictionary: the practice of training people to obey rules or a code of behavior, using punishment to correct disobedience.

For me, it is much more simply put, "this is what I said I was going to do and then I do it.

What happens with most people is they talk about what they are going to do.

You have seen the opposite, or perhaps participated in it?

You decide, "I am going to get up every morning and run, I am going to run every morning, I am committed."
On day two, you look outside and see some rain and say, not today it is raining.

But the person with discipline operates much differently, "I don't care if it is raining, or it is snowing, or it's too hot or too cold. I said I was going to run every day and I am not going to let a little water stop me. I don't care what the weather is. It has nothing to do with my commitment."

Now that is discipline.

I made a commitment to do this and so I have to do it.

Discipline means you do it.

Some additional examples to think about:

You commit that you are going to run a marathon.
Then here comes something that looks like it is going to get in the way.

You say, "I will lose weight."
Then here comes that food I should not eat. What do I do?

You tell the group, I am going back to school.
But I want to sleep not to stay up for two more hours studying all the time.

Success Requires Discipline

One thing you may have learned in the past is that persistence requires discipline. But you will also learn that discipline requires persistence.

"The everyday process of focusing on what you want. And striving for it relentlessly until you get it" Discipline according to Jeffrey Gitomer – Sales Bible.

"The secret of discipline is motivation. When a man is sufficiently motivated, discipline will take care of itself" Alexander Patterson.

Two excellent quotes. How are you doing with discipline in your life, business, career, and family? Do you have it, or don't you have it?

Today, I want to share with you some simple keys to being disciplined. I will share them through the use of an acrostic of the word discipline, what discipline means, and how to make it happen in your life. How do you take control and create greater success in all you do? So, here we go.

D – Decision-making ability.

To be disciplined, you have to be able to make decisions and make them when they need to be made. This is one of those great skills that so few ever get hold of. However, it might just be the most important skill you ever attain.

I learned it in my first real management job. My boss, Nate, was just the best. He did not beat me up for doing the wrong thing, and he did not give me a hard time about what I did. He gave me a hard time about not making a decision. He taught me the principle I have lived and work by since that time in my 20s. Simply put – make a decision. If you make the wrong one, then make another one. At least you are moving. You all know that this is how I operate and try to teach you. It is simply easier and more effective to ask forgiveness than to ask permission.

I – Integrity

The lost art of living and telling the truth. How can you have discipline if you have to keep remembering what is truth and what is not? If you live and work and operate only under the truth, life becomes so much simpler, and discipline becomes so much simpler.

To have great discipline, keep it simple and always tell, live, and work the truth. Try it and see what happens.

S – Shortcuts

Forget shortcuts. Instead, learn to take the narrow road. The wide road, or the road of least resistance, is also the road of least success. That road is not for you. When you get to those forks in life, when you have to make those tough decisions, remember: take the right road, not the easiest road.

This is a major problem today because fewer and fewer people have integrity. We are always looking for the easy way out. We know what has to be done to do the job, but instead of just doing it, we try to find a shortcut. Disciplined people know what has to be done to make it work, and they do it.

C – Character.

Do what you said you were going to do, when you said you were going to do it, the way you said you were going to do it.

"The ability to make yourself do what you should do, when you should do it, whether you feel like it or not" Elbert Hubband.

Imagine the difference when you walk this way.

I – Investor.

To be disciplined, you must be an investor, not a gambler.

When I tell people that it is easier to ask for forgiveness than permission, sometimes, they put that into the realm of gambling. I think it is actually the other way around. You see, by doing nothing, you gamble that it will be OK. Usually, doing nothing makes nothing happen; that is a gamble. Make the investment in taking a risk, in deciding to do. In deciding what you need to do. Then watch what happens.

P – Prepare.

You cannot prepare when it is time to get rolling; it is too late.

For many of us, our moms taught us this simple principle, but as we grew, we thought we knew better – we didn't.

Prepare for what you have to do.

Get the stuff together.

Get what you need to do the job.

Be ready; have it together when the opportunity presents itself.

When you are prepared, you cannot be stopped.

L   Listen.

When you open your ears and shut your mouth, you will be amazed at how different things look. You will be amazed.

Listen to what is going on around you.

Listen to those on your team.

Listen to your inner self.

Then decide and move forward.

I   Initiative

It doesn't just happen, and if you think it does, you are wrong. Make it happen through your action. Stop thinking about it and move forward.

How many are sitting around, still waiting for it to happen?

Too many.

Discipline requires you to do something, to move forward, to make it happen.

N – No.

Busy people don't know how to say no. That is why, instead of being productive, they are busy.

To be disciplined, you have to know how to say "NO."

Be willing to say "NO."

Say "NO."

Think about all the times you got into trouble.

You have too much to do, and because you could not say "no"; now, you have to take shortcuts.

You knew you couldn't do it, but you could not say "no."

You know you shouldn't, but you can't say "no."

Am I getting through? Learn to say no and say "NO."

E – Extra mile.

Disciplined people don't just do it; they do it right. They do more than the minimum.

They go that extra mile.

They do things, but they don't just do them. They do them to the best of their abilities and then even more. Are you ready to do that? Can you do it?

Simple enough, right?

Can you do it?

This week, work these simple steps and watch what happens to your life. Once you learn real discipline, you will be amazed at the results.

So, stop thinking about it, stop hesitating, and get moving.

Build yourself into that very disciplined person, starting today.

If you like this article, then you are going to love the book. This is a chapter from our bestseller:

What's Your Excuse - Everyone's Got One and They All Stink: Winning Means Being Consistent, Persistent and Self-Disciplined

Also, please watch this video on Discipline:

Success Requires Discipline

https://youtu.be/OQTeZ-AvEPw

Chapter 21 exercises

What are you ready to commit to?
What are you going to use that great discipline of your to make happen in your life?

Pick one thing, it can be something as simple as picking up your clothes, I don't care.
What you want to learn is that no matter what, it gets done.

Once you master that.
Then pick one more little thing and do it. Master it.
Then keep repeating this.
You will be amazed at the results you achieve.

For those of you who are consistently late, think about development of the discipline of being early.
As a friend once told me, if you are not early, you are late.

Chapter 22

Morning routine

Don't ask what the world needs. Ask what makes you come alive, and go do it. Because what the world needs is people who have come alive.

Howard Thurman

Let's have some coffee in the morning and enjoy the start of another day.
Let's get up early and enjoy some me time.

Now, you are not going to like my next comment.
But I will encourage each and every one of you starting tomorrow to get up 30 minutes earlier.
Ouch!

I hear you.

The reason I will tell you that it is really simple.
I have been studying entrepreneurs, business owners, and successful people for over 20 years.
People much more successful than me.

But one key element I found in them all, "everybody has a morning routine, and they live hard and fast by it, letting nothing get in the way."

They don't get up and take a shower, throw on some clothes and go to work.

They take time to do something else, something that gets their day rolling the way they want it to.
It can be exercise, reading, meditation.

It is something that they do that they know sets the pace and they do on a regular base, daily.
This is key to the rest of their day.
Get up in control of your day and watch what happens.
Get up proactive and watch what happens.

I know some of you will do this tomorrow and maybe the next day, but a few will make it a regular thing.

But those of you who take this and make it part of your regular day, those are the ones who might just change the world.

Many of you may be on the way to new success in your life.
Add this morning process, and you will have even a great chance for success.
You see, I don't want you to spend those 30 minutes doing just anything, but I want you to spend that time doing something that will develop you.
Physically or mentally.
Something to develop you and help to make you so much more successful.

For me, I get up, and 2 minutes later I am in an exercise program.
But that is my thing.
You have your own.
And it changes as you develop.
I don't do today what I did 3 years ago.

But what I am going to tell you is that when you get up 30 minutes earlier, you will start to see things happening in your life that will amaze you and may put you on a new road to success.

Once you see this happening, you might just think, "perhaps I need to get up another 30 minutes earlier," because you want more of this time.

You begin to see what it is doing to you, and you love it because you are moving at such a higher speed toward your goals.

Yes, to get up earlier requires that you must go to bed earlier.
Yes, you will be tired earlier.
But you will get to bed earlier because you are moving forward toward those goals you want.
You are in control like you have never been before.
And you love it.
You are moving forward toward those goals.
You are doing it.

The morning is a time to exercise, study, read, and work on you.
By the time you get to your regular work, you are pumped up, energized and feeling it.
And everyone is just looking at you and saying, "what happened to you?"

You just smile as you move forward to the life you really want.

My morning routine goes like this:
5:00   Get up, turn on the coffee
5:02   Exercise
5:22   Clean up shave, teeth, wash
5:40   Coffee, read, devotional time
6:40   Breakfast
7:00   Walk
7:30   Daily Live Broadcast and set up
8:00   Write
9:00   Start my other work

Are you Reactive or Pro-active?

Do you make things happen or do you just watch things happen?
Are you taking control of your life or are you watching it go right by you?

These are the questions that we have to ask ourselves every day.

I hope you all know what a pinball machine is. I know it is old school, but I still see them around in most arcades.

A pinball machine has a little silver ball, which is shot up into the machine.
It then bounces from one bumper to the next; it gets pushed.
Then it is flipped from one side to the other; it goes crazy.
It just reacts to all that is happening to it.
It finally just falls into the hole, only to start the process all over again.

How about you?
How about your day?
Do you feel like that pinball?
Are you reactive to an event?
Are you reactive or proactive?

Is this how you are running your life, your business, and your career?
On the other hand, are you pro-active?
Are you the one controlling what you do, how you do it, when you do it?

If you do not start to become more pro-active, then before you know it the next ten years have passed, and you end up where ever instead of where you want to be.
You could go so much further if only you control the process.

Here are seven ways for you to become more pro-active.

1.	Right now.
	Do it right now unless you can't.
	The other day I needed to go to the motor vehicle office.
	It was a simple trip, easy.
	However, did I waste time and energy procrastinating?
	Yes, I did.
	Then finally, I just went, and less than 20 minutes later, it was done.

	Do it right now – try it and watch how much more happens in your life.

2.	Highest Value items.

What are of the highest value and have the most significant success rate in all you do?
Why are you not doing them?
Why are you not finding more and better ways to do them?
If you are in sales, prospecting.
If you are in sales, customer relationships.

Work the highest value items and watch how the rest of the stuff just gets completed.

3. Interruptions.
Stop letting people interrupt you.
You allow it.
You can stop it.
No one else can.
From the people who keep coming in and calling.
To your own self.
From email to the phone.
Stop.
Find a place where you can do things and watch what happens.

If you're able to have two hours of uninterrupted time, then you will do six hours or more of work. Guaranteed.

4. Plan.
Build a plan for the week.
Each day build a plan for the day.
However, the key is neither of those.
The key is, stick to and execute the plan.
Please do not throw it out 35 minutes into the day.
When a fair plan executed, it is of much more value than a great plan not executed.

Please do what you said you were going to do when you said you would do it.

Stop accepting excuses for yourself.

5. Daily.
What are the things you need to do every day?
Put them on a list
Know they have to be done
Get them done.

Salespeople who prospect every day – sell.

6. Stop delaying because you can.
Especially entrepreneurs.
Stop putting it off because you can.
Just do it
Just go and do it now.

The less you put off, the more you will accomplish.

7. Stop thinking about it – start doing it.
How much time did I spend thinking about going to the motor vehicle office?
I have to confess, more than it actually took to do it.

So, just do it.

Follow these few tips and watch what happens to your life, your business, your career.

Want to make this start to happen in your life?
Then please check out our new product, 90 Days to Your Success.
Learn more:
www.90DaystoYourSuccess.com

Chapter 22 exercises

Ok, so now it is your turn.
I want you to get up that ½ earlier, or if you already get up so early, then take the first 30 minutes and dedicate it to a morning routine.

I want you to start easy and slow and pick one thing to do, it can be simply for 10 minutes.
Work to the 30 minutes.
You can do this, and you can be amazing.

Maybe you read a little.
Write something.
Just start
And be consistent.

Once you get into this, you will not let anyone take it away.
I started when my youngest was very little, and she would get up and sit on my lap during as I read.

Now, go and start, it is the first step in action.

Chapter 23

Practice

Immortal question a tourist ask a New York City Cab driver. "How do you get to Carnegie Hall?"
Practice.

Jeffrey Gitomer

How many of you reading this are football fans?
Do you know how much actual play time a regular NFL game has?
I am talking about a time when the players are actually involved in playing the game.
When the players are in action.
Most studies say somewhere between 12-17 minutes.
That is it.
Surprised?

Now since we don't have players who play both offense and defense.
It means that most players have less than 10 minutes of actual action time a week.

Yet how much do they practice and work out?
How much time do they spend on the fundamentals of the game?
They spend all week, most of the day getting ready for this game.
They are working on their game and themselves.
All for less than 10 minutes a week in action.

It is amazing.

When I am getting ready to do a speech, I go through a full practice of the entire speech at least ten times before the day of the actual event. Plus, I usually go through pieces of it many more to make sure they are correct and flow smoothly.
Remember, this is my regular keynote, and I have done this particular speech many, many, many times.
Yet, I practice.
Why?

Well, just like the NFL player, I want to be the best during the time that I have on the field.
A Superstar.
Not just play the game but play the game to win. Play the game to be the best.

Question for you - how much do you practice what you do?

I was already working with a client this morning.
He was working on a video.
I said that the video was really good, but it is not good enough, yet.
He had to keep practicing until he made it almost perfect.
You will never be perfect but trying is the way to become the best.

How long did you practice your skills for over the past week?

You want to keep doing the live stuff, but you also want to spend time on practice.
Make sure you are really good at what you are doing
But not just really good, you want to be the best.

I work with salespeople a great deal.
I always ask them this question, "how much are you practicing your sales skills?"

The answer by most is almost always, "Practice, I been doing this ten years. I don't need no practice."

Yet, when I ask this question of the top players, they almost always say, "Not enough, but I am doing it in the car, on the plane, in my bed, in the line, while I wait. Where ever and whenever I get a chance. I want to be the best at what I do. Many people are very good, but I want to be way ahead of them. I practice all the time and encourage others who are determined to be the best, to practice every day, every chance."

That is why they are the top salespeople.

You want to be at the top of your game; then you need to practice every day.
Practice all you can.
Practice whenever you can.

No matter what you do, practice will make you the best.
From writing to speaking, to keeping books, to answering the phone, to making calls.
In your head, live, as you go to sleep.
Run over and over and over again.
You will be amazed.

When you are the best, everyone else will be amazed.
Wonder how she got that good, must be a natural.

Define "A Natural"
Someone who practices more than anyone else.

Chapter 23 Exercise

Ok, so now you know what you should be doing.
Let's get you on a schedule.
Let's figure out when and how and where you can practice.

First, make a commitment that you want to be the best.

Then commit to practice x number of hours a week.

Then start doing it.
Fundamentals to complex stuff.
Get that good.

Special Note:
Experts have discovered that practice alone isn't enough.

PERFECT practice makes perfect.
That means you need to work with a coach who can objectively critique your practice so when you do practice, you are anchoring in the right things.

To learn more about coaching – check out my video:
What Super Coaching Can Do For You
https://youtu.be/IcSJzy1OQzc

Chapter 24

Listening

This is a cute little story which I found in Our Daily Bread which really hits listening on the head. Remember it is not just about listening in business, but in all of life.

Out of all of the students at a school in Florida, 2550 in total where in trouble

You see a message system notified every parent that their child or children had detention that weekend for bad behavior.

Many kids pleaded their innocence, yet some parents meted out punishment anyway
One mother, Amy admitted that she yelled at her son and made sure he showed up for his detention on Saturday.

To the relief of 2534 kids, and to the embarrassment of some parents, they discovered that the automated message was sent in error to the entire student body when only 16 kids actually deserved detention.

Amy felt so bad about not listening to and believing her son that she took him out for breakfast that Saturday morning.

You see, it seems that as humans we just don't want to take time to listen.

And I know many of you out there could tell even better stories of when you didn't listen.

Yet time and time again, in business and in our lives totally, we find situations where we needed to listen, before we spoke.

Now we come to what I consider the number one skill you need to be a superstar at anything, listening.
We all have to listen, don't we?
God gave us two ears and one mouth, which means that we should be listening twice as much as we talk. Actually, I figure it more to be 80 percent listening, 20 percent talking, or less.

If you want to learn how to succeed you have to learn how to listen.
I teach a great number of salespeople how to listen, and the one thing I tell most all salespeople is you have to learn how to listen.
You have to learn how to be quiet.
You have to learn how to become comfortable in silence.

When I talk about salespeople, I stress the importance of listening.
Remember, everyone in here is a salesperson.
It doesn't matter that you don't sell outside, you still have people to sell to.

You have to sell your ideas, your concepts, your concerns about what you want to accomplish.
You have to get someone to move forward with you and support you.
You might have to get someone to accomplish something for you, getting things done through others.

You have to sell your boss on your idea.
You have to sell your spouse on the concept.
You even have to sell your children on things.
That is why I tell people to read sales books, whether or not we are in sales, we all have to sell.

Now if you take enough time to listen, there is an interesting concept of listening which says, "if I listen well and long enough, the person will decide to buy themselves.
They will say OK.
They will buy it.

He who talks first loses.
Hard to teach, but so powerful.
Learn to be the last one to talk, and most all your needs will get be done.

If I converse with you, then you will be doing 80% of the talking.
Then when our conversation is finished, you will turn around and tell others, "Manny is really great to talk with."

But guess who did almost all the talking?

Learn that people love to talk.
Fact.
People love to talk about themselves.
Fact.
If you listen, you will really build a strong relationship, and you will be amazed at the results.

Leadership Means Listening To What Is Not Being Said

You're a bus driver and your heading south with 55 passengers.
Leg one of the trip, 4.4 miles and turn east.
Leg 2 – 3.3 miles
Leg 3 Turn back south 2.2 miles
Leg 4 Turn East 1.1 miles
You've driven 2 directions but made three turns for 4 different legs. 4.4+3.3+2.2+1.1 = 11 miles.
Question: How old is the bus driver?

You are the bus driver – how old are you?
When someone is trying to take your focus off – get it back.
Zig Ziglar

https://youtu.be/beVekqvmABA

How often do we pride ourselves on being great listeners, yet we just blow stuff off?

As leaders, we all have a full plate, stuff overflowing – but we have to remember that our people are what matters most. Without them, we will not create anywhere near what we are capable of.

Today I want to share 3 keys that will make you a better leader.

1/   How many times has someone told you that something bothers them, really bothers them, but you just blew them off? Then, they end up leaving your organization, and you sit there wondering why. But they tell everyone else, "this was bugging me, I tried to get the boss to see it, but he/she just didn't listen."

Great leadership requires great listening and taking action. Make sure you become aware of those things that are getting under the skin of your team and do something about them.

2/   How many times has everyone, but you known that a person in your organization is not what you think they are? Yet your mind is made up, and you ignore their objections and keep rolling. Companies have lost money, good people and great opportunities because the leader did not listen to those, he/she should trust the most. Keep these communication lines open, and make sure your team is not afraid to tell you the truth.

A long time ago, I learned the hard way that a prospect should never come ahead of a customer. The same applies here: the new guy/girl (the one who you believe can walk on water) should not come ahead of those you trust and who have helped you get there so much in the past.

3/   When you mess up, stop, admit it, and clear the air. As leaders, we often do little stupid stuff, which we just blow off, but this can create a wall that stops us from ever earning the maximum performance of our players.

I remember giving a chair to one of my sales people in our old office. Later, when we moved to our new office, I took it back and used it myself, never saying anything. Not that big a deal, right? I wasn't able to put that relationship right again until I sucked it up and admitted how stupid I was. Be careful, the little stuff does really matter. Maybe not to you, but to someone.

Leaders, open your mind and listen this week. Take a look around and see if any of these apply to you and your team. If so, do what you need to make it right. You might be amazed by the results.

Chapter 25

One Final Story
Adversity

"Hardships often prepare ordinary people for an extraordinary destiny."

C.S. Lewis

Let me leave you with a story of adversity.
This story is about adversity, as adversity often gets in our way and holds us back.

I don't know who first told the story or who gets the credit for it, but I heard it, and I am passing it on.

There is this young lady, and she comes into her grandfather's restaurant.
The grandfather is in the kitchen, so she joins him there.

She says, "PopPop, I cannot do this anymore. I am going crazy. Please help me.
I can't get to where I want to go.
I can't accomplish what I want to do.
It is just too much for me; I think I shall just quit."

The grandfather was a wise man, and he said to his granddaughter.
Please get me three pots and fill them with water.
Then put them on the stove and turn the temperature to high.
She did.

In a little bit the water in each began to boil.

PopPop as she called him, then he said to her.
"Take these potatoes and put them in the first pot." She did.
"Takes these eggs, and be very careful with them, and put them in the second pot." She did.
"Then take these coffee beans and put them in the third pot." She did.

Now after about 30 minutes passed, he says to her, let's us go back and examine each pot.

Together they look at the first pot, the one containing the potatoes.
The grandfather says, "see these potatoes, they were so hard when you put them in the pot, but now after 30 minutes in the boiling water, they are mush."

I want to relate this to you. This is just like you if you let adversity make you quit and hold you back. If you allow this, you too will become, just as the potatoes, mush."

Then they continued to the second pot.
The one with the eggs. The grandfather then says, "remember I told you to be careful with the eggs because they were very fragile. If you dropped them before they when into the boiling water, they would break into pieces.
If you examine them now, you will see that they are very hard.

When dealing with an adversarial relationship you too can become hard like the eggs, and that will not help you move any further than becoming mush like the potatoes.

Neither mush or hard can help you with adversity."

Now the third pot, and it is always the third in any story isn't it.
That is how we develop stories when I teach speakers or writers.

When you look at the coffee beans in the third pot, they really don't look any different than when they went into the boiling water.
But instead, the boiling water has changed.
The water has become that great drink we call coffee.
The coffee beans turned the boiling water into coffee.
The boiling water did not affect the coffee beans; it was the other way around; the coffee beans turned the boiling water into coffee.

This is how you handle adversity.
Change things you have to deal with every day.

The question on the table to you the reader.
Where you are?
Where you are going?
What is next?

It is all under your control.
But you have to take that control.
You have to be as the coffee beans and change the process not like the potatoes or the eggs.

Chapter 26

Conclusion

The price of success is much lower than the price of failure.

Zig Ziglar

Stop Limiting Yourself
When you are born, ever one believes there is no limit to what this child can do.

But then you spend the next 22 years having limits imposed upon you.
All that training finally gets you to the point where you start putting limits on yourself
Then the cycle begins again.

Never Put a limit on Your Dreams
Dreams are supposed to be limitless.
If you put limits on your dreams, they are just thoughts; they are not dreaming.
Dream big.
Dream strong.
Dream consistently.

Stretch Yourself
Until you almost break.
Then heal and go right back to it.
No one ever achieved greatness without stretching themselves.
Take a look

Remove Your Limits
How fast would you drive if there weren't any speed limits?
Who is putting limits on you?

Why?

Is it you, because you tried and failed and will never try again?
Is it them, because they don't want you to be any greater than they are?
Is it others, because they fear to lose you as a friend if you succeed?

Limits are good if used correctly.
But they stop most people from ever achieving their full potential.
God didn't put us here to be held back.

To find your true self and all you are capable of, you have to be willing to live without the opinions of others

Opinions are like old garbage...

Everyone has one, and they all stink.
Not that feedback is not important, but feedback is not opinion.

A great story that my friend Richard, a successful business builder and MLM champion told me many years ago.

"Those things, (MLM) don't work.
Then why are there people making millions of dollars doing it?
Trouble is the person telling you that is someone who once tried it, then gave up and swore that they would never to try it again.'

I have tried it five times and failed every one.
Will I try it again, given the right opportunity, of course!
Will I tell you not to try it – never.
But I will share what I learned.

Just Do it
I have given you all you need up to now.

Now you have only to do it.

The final frontier.
The one so few goes out to, and even few get across.

Are you going to be one of those who never take the shot?
Chances are if you got to this part of the book – you are going to do it.
Most people gave up chapters ago.
If you are still reading, then you are ready to rock.

Much success to you in all you do.
Thank you for reading this book.

Please give us a review on Amazon.

And please share your experiences and your successes with me.
I would love to hear how you do.

Thanks,

Coach Manny Nowak

Here is my connection data and some of the tools you can work with today.

90 Days to Your Success.
Double Your Sales
Coach Manny Private Facebook group – The Entrepreneur Toolbox

Website:
www.CoachManny.com

Facebook Page:
www.facebook.com/manny.nowak

Linkedin Profile:
www.linkedin.com/in/mannynowak/

Products:

90 Days to Your Success
http://coachmanny.com/90-days-to-your-success/

Double Your Sales Course
http://coachmanny.com/double-your-sales/

Coach Manny's private Facebook group: The Entrepreneur Toolbox
http://coachmanny.com/coach-mannys-inner-circle/

Hire Manny to speak at Your next event:
http://coachmanny.com/need-a-speaker/

Interested in having Manny as your coach?
http://coachmanny.com/business-results-coaching-2/

Other Books by Coach Manny
http://coachmanny.com/books-by-coach-manny/

Free Courses from Coach Manny:
http://coachmanny.com/free-courses-from-coach-manny/

www.ingramcontent.com/pod-product-compliance
Lightning Source LLC
Chambersburg PA
CBHW021942170526
45157CB00003B/890